Personal Boundaries for Highly Sensitive People

A Simple Practice for Self-Care in Moments of Conflict

Grace Kerina

Grace Kerina – gracekerina.com

Published by Shine Even If (Eugene, Oregon, USA) – shineevenif.com

ISBN 978-1-7342493-6-1 (ebook) | ISBN 978-1-7342493-7-8 (paperback)

Cover design by Ebook Launch (ebooklaunch.com)

Interior illustrations by Grace Kerina

Proofread by Anna Paradox

First edition

The advice and strategies contained herein may not be suitable for your situation. You should consult with a professional when appropriate.

Acknowledgments: Thanks to PKW, who gently demonstrated clear but firm boundaries all those years ago and got me thinking. Thanks also to Carrie McCarthy for stepping into the first boat, and to Lauren Sapala for acceptance and support.

To our younger selves, with love and respect.
They did their best, always.

Contents

Introduction

When someone says, "I'm not comfortable with this right now," they're stating a personal boundary. Your personal boundaries are limits beyond which you don't want to go. That simple definition introduces an empowering concept with many applications in everyday life.

Boundaries are personal. What feels like an uncomfortable or threatening interaction to one person might not even faze another person. How you're affected by interactions with others and how you choose to respond depend on factors like who you are, how you grew up, what's at stake, and how accustomed you are to standing up for yourself.

Healthy boundaries have everything to do with holding on to yourself while interacting with others, even during differences of opinion. If you're feeling overwhelmed or overloaded, you may opt to either be your authentic self *or* interact with someone, but not do both at once. This book and the 9 Steadying Points offer a basic system for gently building the skill of holding on to your true self *while* interacting with others. This is the process of *differentiation*, which I think of as the practice of *allowing differences*.

The benefits to be gained from holding personal boundaries and allowing differences can last a lifetime and add up to more satisfying, deeper, and more intimate relationships, starting with your relationship with yourself. Self-respect, self-esteem, and increased inner calmness are a few of the outcomes people experience with shipshape boundaries in place.

Sensing with Sensitivity

In my decades of supporting highly sensitive people, writers, artists, intuitives, empaths, and introverts, I've often witnessed the obstacles and rewards of living an authentic life as a sensitive person. I embody all of the characteristics in that list and have experienced obstacles and rewards myself as well. Because the word *sensitive* has multiple associations, some of which are used as snubs ("You're too sensitive"), I like to bring in the word *sensing*, which can have less charge for some people. We are highly *sensing* people. We sense the world with sensitivity.

An authentic, creative, fulfilled life hinges on connecting to and protecting your internal sense of self-truth. Creativity hugely benefits from healthy personal boundaries, which support the claiming of space and time in which to focus and learn, and the freedom to choose inspiring environments and community.

As someone who automatically and empathically tunes in to what others are feeling, I've learned to pay special attention to my own boundaries. For a long time I didn't, because I didn't know what boundaries were or how they could help me. I *did* know life seemed easier when I didn't make waves, but then, not making waves limited my interactions with others. Not interacting kept me from helping people in some of the ways I really wanted to, and kept me from developing a community I felt comfortable with. I realized I needed a healthy way to engage with people, a way that worked even when interactions got tense for me. I needed a way to be true to myself *with* people, and I found it.

What Is a Steadying Point?

The essence of a *practice* is *action*. But even before taking action, awareness is needed about which action to practice and when. Breaking down the personal boundary process into separate moments, or *points*, of awareness, can make taking action more manageable.

For example, the first of the 9 Steadying Points is simply to notice that something feels off during an interaction. That's all. Each Point offers an opportunity to dial in and realize there's a steadying action you could take toward being your authentic self while you're interacting with someone.

Practicing the Points helps you identify potential problem areas, strengthen your skills, gain flexibility, and increase your options around personal boundaries. Having this system to lean into in the moment can make all the difference. Practice the 9 Steadying Points enough and you bake in these healthy habits, making self-support easier and more immediate.

Try any of the Steadying Points and you'll gain awareness. Start small. Go easy. No rush. Use the Points to calm yourself, to build inner trust that you *can* take care of yourself, and to interact with more confidence. The goal is not a perfect state of personal boundaries nirvana, but a grasp of tools with which you can build the life you want. I've been practicing these Points for many years and still use them frequently.

Your Own Little Boat

This compact book is not meant to be comprehensive. It's more of a back-pocket guide to grab when you're in the moment and need a reminder or a boost of courage.

To inject some fun and make the Points easier to remember, this guide is packed with nautical imagery and metaphors, which fit beautifully with the issue of boundaries. Through the simple device of associating personal boundaries with boats on water, the mind can be nudged into tossing out life-preserver reminders in moments when clear thinking is elusive.

For example, if you imagine that having healthy personal boundaries is like sitting calmly in your own little boat, you're more likely to recognize a boundary challenge when someone like a pushy client or a bullying family member tries to stick their big boot into your boat. *Tippy. Not good. Obvious.*

Within this nautical framework, each Point includes a key question to ask yourself. Many of the Points apply to the first few minutes, or even seconds, of a potential boundary situation. Even just remembering the question for a Point in a situation can help.

Each Point is explained in detail, with a focus on straightforward directions for how to take action. The final Point (Point 9) offers specific tools and support for automation and mastery, with suggestions for how to preprogram the Points to make them more readily available to you when your personal boundary alarm goes off.

At the end of the book, you'll find directions for accessing a handy reminder tool in different formats, to further encourage your practice of the 9 Steadying Points.

You Are in Charge of You

It's important to know that managing your boundaries doesn't always mean taking action. Depending on the circumstances and your sense of what's true for you, your response from a place of personal integrity might be to do nothing, to hold back, to be quiet. A benefit of working with the 9 Steadying Points is an increased internal awareness and clarity about what to do or *not* do around holding a personal boundary.

This boundary work is a reclamation of self. You are in charge of you. That's a big responsibility, but self-responsibility is where self-empowerment lives. You decide about your own life.

During the process of deciding what manner of boundaries to establish, take into account the likely actions and reactions of the people you're dealing with. If setting a boundary is likely to bring on physical recriminations, emotional abuse, or other endangerment to you or those in your care, the most effective and healthy boundary you could create might be one of distance—of disengaging or leaving altogether.

The specifics of what to do in such cases is beyond the scope of this book. If you find yourself in such circumstances, consider reaching out for advice and support from professionals or organizations who will be on your side and who have the expertise to help you figure out how to be safe.

Every attempt you make to practice healthy personal boundaries counts and accrues. Just *begin*. I'm rooting for you. I believe in your ability to give that crusty anchor a yank so you can get more of what you really want out of life and take your whole self along for the ride.

Now, steady yourself with a hand on either side of your boat. Off we go.

Chapter 1
Point 1: Check the Weather

"What's rocking my boat?"

How do you know when a boundary goes awry? What alerts you? The sooner you notice the warning signs, the easier it is to begin to steady yourself, and the more time you have to decide what to do. Point 1 is just about *noticing* that something feels off.

This Point may seem like a no-brainer, but it's not merely about nodding yes to acknowledge a weird feeling. Point 1's power is in the development of your personal discretion. In the case of boundaries, being able to discern whether or not a disturbance in the local weather is a boundary problem or not is key, because not all situations in which you feel discomfort will necessarily have to do with boundaries. Try to pinpoint the source of the disturbance in your environment so you can gain clarity about this. Where is the disturbance coming from? From a particular person? From particular words spoken? From a physical gesture? An implication? Use your internal radar.

Your uniqueness extends to the ways in which you notice that your boundaries are being pushed. Different people experience different warning signs and different constellations of warning signs. You may know some of yours already. By paying attention to what you're feeling when you're in a situation that *obviously* threatens your boundaries (or by reviewing the experience afterward), you'll learn more about your own warning signs. Whenever you can clarify those feelings, it will help you fine-tune your threat-recognition abilities so you can notice boundary issues sooner.

Often, signs of boundary problems arise both internally and externally. You feel icky *and* someone is yelling in your face. The icky feeling is internal. The yelling is external. Familiarity with both kinds of signs is useful in helping to hone your ability to recognize your personal boundary-breach warning alerts.

The purpose of the lists of warning signs below is to give you examples to consider as you discover and fine-tune your experience and knowledge of *your own* warning signs. There are plenty of other possible signs besides the ones listed here.

If the idea appeals to you, create lists of your internal and external signs as you practice Point 1. You could stash your lists on your phone for handy reference in the moment.

Examples of Internal Warning Signs

It's important to know that the signs listed below do not always signal boundary problems. This is where the discretion skills of Point 1 come in. Anxiety, for instance, isn't always about having a boundary threatened. Sometimes anxiety is about not having gotten enough sleep, or getting a phone call from the hospital, or walking into a room full of people you've never met.

Think of each warning sign you discover and recognize in yourself as a tool tailor-made for you, a personalized alert to help you discover what might need your attention in your environment.

The signs are listed in rough order of intensity level, from milder to more intense.

- Fuzzy thinking
- Confusion
- Difficulty maintaining your own perspective (switching to someone else's perspective)
- Feeling that things are moving too quickly
- Increased anxiety
- Apprehension about speaking your truth
- Overwhelm
- Irritability
- Hurt feelings
- Defensiveness
- Impatience
- Anger
- Fear

Be aware that a feeling that your boundaries are threatened may not have to do with anyone else in your current situation. For instance, sometimes our boundaries are troubled by events or people in the present that remind us of our own past problems. This is another reason to develop Point 1's skill of discretion. Be wary of rushing mistakenly to the conclusion that someone else is the trigger of your boundary warning. First, rule out internal causes, which will help you avoid inappropriate reactions to your warning signs. Practice is your friend. Don't expect to get healthy boundaries perfectly right from the start. Grant yourself patience. If you experience too much internal confusion to sort this out on your own, consider getting help from a good counselor.

Examples of External Warning Signs

When someone else's behavior pings your boundary alert, that's an external warning. External events prompt internal reactions. You'll notice in the list below that the words for external warning signs (someone else's behavior) can be the same as for internal warning signs (what you feel).

Depending on who you are, it's possible to be faced with some of the external signs below and *not* feel as though a boundary is being threatened. It depends on who you are, what your strengths are, your history, your support network, your experience and level of mastery in various situations, and a host of other factors.

Here in Point 1 the goal is to develop your discretion muscles. The more aware you are of the internal and external factors at play in your life, the greater the chance you'll be able to recognize boundary threats when they happen to *you*.

Here are some examples of behaviors from others, from external sources, that might register in you as warnings. Feel free to make your own list.

- Irritability
- Unsolicited criticism
- Disrespect
- Defensiveness
- Interrupting
- Dominating the conversation
- Pressure for you to conform against your wishes
- Pressure for you to make a decision when you've said you're not ready to
- Impatience
- Sharp voice
- Raised voice
- Contempt
- Anger
- Escalating negative emotion
- Threatening physical behavior
- Actual physical behavior

If you're in the vicinity of someone else's threatening or actual physical behavior that is setting off your alarms, first up is getting support, which is beyond this guide to provide. You deserve all the help you need.

The practice of Point 1: Check the Weather may only take a few seconds, which is fine. Other times, you may have a vague feeling of unease that takes a while to zero in on. Each situation will come with its own weather and timing. At the first sign of a squall on the horizon or an unsettling wind, pay attention, tune in, and sharpen up.

Chapter 2
Point 2: Stay in Your Own Boat

"Am I sitting by myself in my own boat?"

The practice of healthy boundaries requires that in a challenged situation, you view the situation from your own perspective. Extending understanding and empathy to others to the point of losing track of yourself won't do. It distorts the view, like looking through the wrong end of a telescope. Reeling in the perspective doesn't mean being cold or blind to others and what they're going through. It does mean, however, that when your goals conflict with someone else's, centering yourself is crucial. Point 2 is all about making sure you're seeing things from your own perspective.

When your boundaries feel compromised, get into your own boat and sit down.

Imagining that everyone involved in the current situation has their own boat is a way to practice noticing what's going on. If you've been on any kind of floating device, even an inner tube in the backyard pool, you have a reference point for getting through Point 2. Look around. Who is doing flying cannonballs into the center of the discussion, splashing everyone? Who has a foot stuck over into someone else's boat? Who is trying to walk on water, confused about the boundary basics of being at sea in a boat? Who is careening around with a motor on the back of their boat, making dangerous waves and causing havoc? And who is sitting down, in sole control of their own little boat, all limbs present and accounted for? Hopefully, that's you. With a little imagination, using this Point 2 tool can reveal a lot about your circumstances and provide useful insights.

The purpose of Point 1 is to recognize that a boundary threat might be happening. Here in Point 2, you secure your own self. If your limbs are in someone else's boat, retrieve them. Sit down and look around at the scene from the vantage point of your very own perspective.

The practice of Point 2: Stay in Your Own Boat is straightforward and simple, but crucial.

Chapter 3
Point 3: Stop Rowing

"Have I stowed my oars?"

What happens when you're on alert? After practicing Point 2, you may be sitting alone in your own boat, but that doesn't guarantee access to your brain's wisdom. Maybe you're flooded with emotion. Your thoughts may be scrambled. Head buzzing. Palms sweaty. Not sure what to do, if anything. Yikes!

These first few Steadying Points often take place over a very short span of time: *Yup, I've got a boundary problem*

(Point 1). *Okay, I've pulled my awareness back to my own perspective, even though my heart is racing* (Point 2).

The immediate next thing to practice, here in Point 3, is to quit trying to go anywhere. (An exception is if you're in real danger and need to leave the scene to be safe.) Point 3 is about diminishing input. Stop rowing. Stop talking, stop whimpering, stop trying to make things better for everyone or anyone else, stop trying to defend your position, stop huffing. Just *stop*. Your goal here is to allow even a *bit* more space in which to breathe and be—to calm your nervous system and remember who you really are, as preparation for beginning the process of thinking.

In Point 3, you stop making things actually or potentially worse and you contain yourself to a place where you can begin to figure out what to do from here.

Use steadying actions to gain self-access, which is like deploying pontoons to stabilize your own boat, thereby extending the space that's yours with protective flotation devices.

Examples of Steadying Actions

The options listed below are *actions*, meaning they're things to physically *do*. This is important because connecting with yourself physically helps with getting centered. Experiment to learn which actions work best for you in your Point 3 moments. Some of these actions may work better than others at different times and in different situations. Zero in on your own personalized list of what's effective, and be on the lookout for additional examples.

- Close your mouth

- Blink a few times
- Take a step or two backward
- Sit back in your chair instead of leaning forward
- Push your chair back to gain some distance
- Bend down and re-tie or brush off your shoes
- Stretch
- Sit up straighter
- Put both feet flat on the floor
- Wiggle your toes
- Roll your head around to stretch your neck
- Roll your shoulders
- Hold your own hand for reassurance and self-support
- Pat your chest or your belly
- Take a drink of water
- Tilt your notebook against the edge of the table like a shield
- Doodle hearts on your notepad
- Close your eyes
- Take a deep breath in through your nose and let it out through your mouth; do it again
- Tighten then relax your hands or any other tense body parts
- Notice what parts of your body feel disconnected and reconnect them
- Look away into the distance
- Hug yourself
- Smile secretly to yourself
- Keep breathing deep breaths

When you practice Point 3: Stop Rowing, you shift your perspective to the physical, to remembering that you can be present in your body. You can calm your own self, even a little, and gain the power of space. Tunnel vision gives way to a view of the horizon. The sirens fade to silence. Overwhelm diminishes.

As you sit more calmly in your little boat, take a few moments to notice the difference.

Chapter 4
Point 4: Get Your Bearings

"Where am I in relation to where I want to be?"

Now that you've noticed that a boundary problem exists (Point 1), paid attention to pulling your awareness back to your own perspective (Point 2), and taken action to settle more into your body (Point 3), it's time to expand your mental space for decision-making with Point 4.

The practice at this Point is to check in and get your bearings until you can think more clearly. Depending on the situation, you may have gone a long way toward accomplishing this by getting through Point 3. Being quiet and taking deep breaths can sometimes right you if you notice what's going on early enough and if the stakes are not too high or the situation too threatening. But sometimes Point 3's steadying actions are not enough.

One way to help yourself get your bearings is to physically go somewhere else—somewhere you can be alone with yourself, even for just a few moments. For example, if you excuse yourself and retreat to the bathroom, you can take a minute to look at yourself in the mirror and say hello. You can review the Steadying Points and remind yourself that you have a plan for self-care in times of conflict. You can give yourself a pep talk in private.

If you don't want to leave the situation that triggered your boundary alarm, there are other ways of expanding your thinking space. In a meeting, for example, you could write a note to yourself that no one else can see, jotting down things to help you connect with your authentic self. *Hi, me. I'm feeling uncomfortable because the boss keeps adding things to my to-do list that I didn't agree to and I'm not saying no and everyone is looking at me. To slow myself down, I'm going to keep taking deep breaths and just sit here in my own boat and hold on until my shoulders relax. Then I'll make a plan.*

It's a good idea at this point to ask yourself the HALT questions. Used in twelve-step and other programs to remind people of stressors, the acronym HALT stands for *hungry, angry, lonely,* or *tired.* Are you any of those? Or do you have to pee? Are you distracted by worry about something that has nothing to do with the situation that tweaked your boundary alarm? If so, can you alleviate any of those issues quickly to take them off your plate and clear up more space (like eating a quick snack)?

Acknowledge whatever may be pulling on your attention

besides the boundary issue at hand. Otherwise, you may bring complications into the boundary situation that don't belong here. It can be helpful to try to deal with only one thing at a time. Your nervous system will thank you.

Another way to get your bearings is to remind yourself why you're in this particular situation. *I'm here in this interview to get information so I can decide if I want to attend this college. Or I'm here at this party to see if there's anyone in this group I might like enough to want to be friends with. Or I'm here at this dinner with my parents-in-law to support my wife and to practice the art of tolerance.* Clarity here will serve you well during the next two Points.

The main objective in Point 4 is to strengthen a feeling of connection with your true self, calm in your own boat. There are many ways to get your bearings, and you may already know the best way for you. If not, try a variety of things to discover what works for you. Pay attention to which self-connection methods work for you in general, and which ones work best for you in different situations. Once you've found one or two methods that work, don't stop looking. Add to your repertoire so that in the moments you need them, you'll have multiple options for getting your bearings.

In Point 4: Get Your Bearings, you've gained more thinking room and identified and dealt with distractions. Next up is experimentation. Steady on.

Chapter 5
Point 5: Test the Water

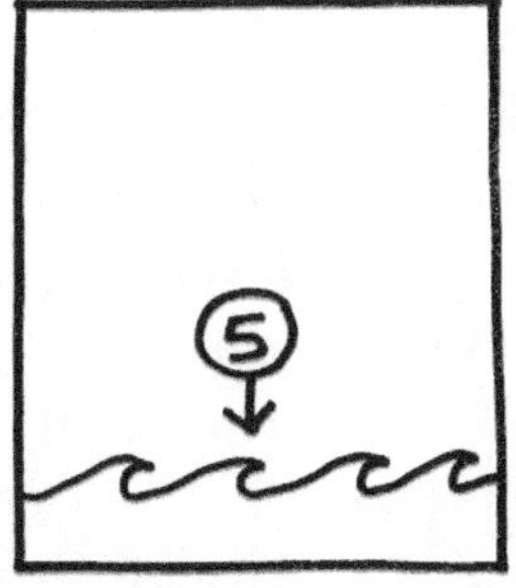

"What's a small test I can do?"

Point 5 is about taking a healthy action to claim a boundary, as a small test, *and paying attention to how you feel as a result.* The aim is to succeed on a tiny level to give yourself courage to do more. Remain cautious if you like. That's totally fine. There will be no shoving here.

To do a real-world trial run of your boundary-holding skills, stick the tip of your oar into the water only enough to get the feel of it in your hands. No need to lean in and tense your muscles for a big push yet. Just dip and notice what happens inside you. That's all.

Let's say you're having lunch with your sister and she's assuming, as usual, that you'll deal with all the preparations for the holiday bash for the whole extended family. When she slides a long shopping list to you across the kitchen table, your boundary alarm goes off. Remembering to practice the Steadying Points, you close your mouth and excuse yourself to take a break in the bathroom, where you notice your panicked look in the mirror. You wash your hands longer than usual because the warm water feels good and helps you calm down. One big breath in, exhale, and you acknowledge the fact that you're not up for taking responsibility for the holiday celebration *again* this year.

Now that you've gotten a better grip on yourself and on your goal in this situation with your sister, it's time to dip an oar into the water and do a test to practice holding your boundary: one little baby dip, one different action from usual, a healthy and small act. *Then pay attention to the inner result.*

You return to the kitchen, sit down, and push the list back to your sister's side of the table. That was your test. Notice how you *feel* as a result. *Whoa. My arm trembled as I pushed that list away, but it also feels so good to not automatically say yes, for once, just to please her.* You did it! That is a completely worthwhile practice of Point 5.

Point 5 is *not* about changes that result in the external situation. How someone else reacts or doesn't react to your little test is not the focus of Point 5. The important thing is to identify the *feeling* of being true to yourself within a situation where you identified a need and took an action to hold a boundary.

Here's another example. Perhaps you're having a heated discussion with your wife. Your boundary alarm goes off as your pulse rate and her voice both rise. You notice this shift in the weather and excuse yourself to step into the backyard and get your bearings. While there, you clarify your goal for the situation and realize that remaining connected with your friend who is also your wife is your top priority, even more important than winning this emotionally charged argument right now. You walk back to the den and don't say anything. You look her in the eye and do one small thing differently: You smile. *And then you pay attention to how you feel as a result.*

Keep testing. Keep trying different ways of making small forays toward more authentic expression. Practice enough and it will get easier to identify the feeling of being true to yourself while holding a personal boundary. It's fine if this practice of Point 5 takes a while, if it takes more than a few tries in more than a few situations, and even if it takes a long while. There's no "right" timeline. Whatever happens is perfectly okay. You're building a muscle. Being able to recognize and hold on to your true self during uneasy interactions is a valuable skill, but you may be starting from scratch. *Your* best results will come from letting yourself be yourself, without judgment or pressure to be otherwise.

In some circumstances, dipping an oar into the water as you practice Point 5 may reveal that you're already in deeper water than you'd expected and your boundary alarm went off because you're too far out of your depth. It could be that this is neither the time nor the situation in which to take a stand or to try even a small test. You may realize that the healthiest thing for you to do now is leave the situation immediately. If this is the case, skip the next point, Point 6, and move directly to Point 7: Head for Shore. Sometimes a healthy boundary is best set by removing yourself altogether so you can regroup and get centered over a longer period of time, during which you can consider the benefits of enlisting skilled support.

Here at Point 5: Test the Water, if your oar-dip experiments resulted in *any* degree of feeling more authentic, or gave you even a small sense of self-loving satisfaction, no matter what happened externally, then you've managed to increase the stability and security of your own boat. You're building healthy skills, one dip at a time.

Chapter 6
Point 6: Ride the Wave

"Am I steering my own boat as I ride the wave?"

When your oar-dip test in Point 5 isn't enough to resolve a personal boundaries situation, you may be confronting Point 6. If you're aware that more is needed in order to assert your boundary *and* you're feeling safe enough with the risk, it's time to try riding a bigger wave.

The key practice in Point 6 is building self-trust around assessing circumstances. Is this particular boundary-holding experiment a risk you're willing and able to take at this particular time? Do you feel safe enough about the possible ways this experiment might turn out? Do you know what you want to say or do (or *not* say or *not* do), and do you feel confident enough about staying safely in your own boat in the process? Are you ready to commit to this bigger boundary declaration, even if only for a limited time, and even if you get splashed in the process?

In Point 6, there's some uncertainty about how things will turn out, but you've assessed the risk to be low enough for you to handle, so you're ready to lean in and row up the face of the wave.

As you consider potential risks and take action, keep asking yourself questions. What are you feeling? What do you hope to accomplish as an outcome? What part of you are you wanting to protect? Who is rocking your boat? What do they want? Where is your boundary?

At a work meeting, you swallow hard and say, "I'd like to offer another perspective." Everyone at the conference table turns to stare at you. You plant both feet firmly on the floor, sit up straight, and speak into the silence. "There aren't enough positives in this proposal. If we accept it, we'll be fending off problems for too long before we see any benefits. I suggest we look at other proposals instead."

When you express your true self, you crest a wave. Inhale and exhale as you slide down the other side. Take note of people's responses, but focus on the reassuring comfort of staying in your own perspective. The person or people you're interacting with will have whatever reactions they have. Their reactions are their responsibility. What do *you* need in this moment? How do *you* want to respond?

When we make moves to practice healthy boundaries, we may disrupt the status quo enough to set a push-back effect in motion, particularly in situations where we've historically behaved with less self-assertion. That first bigger wave may lead to another. *Breathe.* Do whatever you can to stay in your own boat, which is exactly where you belong. What is happening inside you? How connected can you remain with a feeling of being in tune with yourself?

Three Powerful Wave-Rider Tools

I've discovered three specific and powerful tools for navigating Point 6's waves: 1) tell the truth anyway, 2) forget finesse, and 3) whose responsibility is it?

These are not always *easy* tools to use, but there's an element of magic to them, and they definitely become easier with practice. If you're willing to experiment with them, you'll develop a sense of how and when to use one or another of these life-preserver tools in situations when you need to ride a wave to hold a boundary.

Tell the Truth Anyway – In a situation where you think someone else may be disappointed if you share who you really are, telling your truth anyway can be freeing for you both—you get to regain your internal integrity and the other person gets the opportunity to update their expectations. Consider if you want to prepare or plan ahead, or if a particular delivery system appeals to you—in person, email, letter, video call, with the support of a therapist, through mediation, etc. Or you may blurt your truth anyway in a surprise moment when doing so feels right.

If, in the past, you didn't tell the truth, and someone developed false expectations about you as a result, you can include an apology when you set the record straight, if you deem it appropriate. Be aware that there may be back-spray as others make adjustments. As always, your safety is the first priority. After using this tool of telling the truth anyway, be on the lookout for a feeling of relief due to increased internal alignment.

Forget Finesse – This tool is about prioritizing integrity over image when you feel like you have to choose one or the other in order to speak up for yourself. If the outcome is more important than how you get there, consider bumbling. Forgetting finesse can get you through to the other side when you just want to get a tough interaction over with.

Assess the situation before you toss aside finesse. If you're in a job or role that includes maintaining a certain degree of finesse, take that into consideration. In many cases, though, holding tight to a goal of *doing it right* or *pulling it off without a hitch* can seriously impair a competing goal of expressing integrity (telling the truth). Yes, you can stumble over your words, let your voice warble, stutter, back up and start over, cry as you talk, fumble with your notes, *and keep going*. I've done this many times and I know many other people who have as well. It's very freeing.

Whose Responsibility Is It? – Answering or even attempting to answer this question has untangled many fraught relationship knots. Sorting out who is responsible for what in an upsetting situation takes stock of whose feet are in whose boat. The key to this tool is accepting that 1) the only feet you can control are your own and 2) you don't have control over anyone else's feet. So when someone comes at you with disappointment that you didn't do something they expected you to, you can do an internal responsibility check. Did you promise them something you didn't deliver on? If not, are they upset about an expectation they created without your agreement? In that case, use your imaginary oar to lift their heavy feet out of your boat. Not your problem.

Here's an example of using all three of these wave-rider tools: A woman tells you she's attracted to you, but you don't feel the same way about her. From experience, you know that if you don't apply the brakes now, the situation will become more difficult later on, so you take a big breath and say, "I appreciate the courage it's taken for you to tell me your feelings, but I... there's a..." Your voice started out strong, but suddenly became weak and wobbly. "I mean, you... you're... It's not... um...." Distressed by how hard it feels to disappoint her, you break eye contact and start to panic, but then you remember about boats. With a deep inhale, you reach for the sides of your own boat. You remind yourself that your truth matters, even if she gets upset. After an awkward silence, you stare at your feet and push out the final words. "Well, I just don't feel that way about you." Your heart is about to pound out of your shirt, but you did it, you removed her uninvited leg from your boat. When you dare to look up, she seems mad, and says some things in a loud voice. When she heads off in a huff, tears in her eyes, it's an option to let her go. She's got her own work to do to adjust to a new perspective (and she may or may not do that work). But *you* did *your* work, and that is something you can definitely be proud of.

The process of holding healthy boundaries often requires expectations to be adjusted—your expectations about yourself and about other people, and other people's expectations about you and themselves. This may require uncomfortable or painful shifts in order to come into alignment with reality. Although this process is not always pretty, the benefits are magnificent. The rewards of smoother sailing and internal alignment are far-reaching and worth the effort.

Point 6: Ride the Wave is about making the brave choice to be authentic even when the seas are rough. As you practice this Point, you find your sea legs and gain confidence.

Chapter 7
Point 7: Head for Shore

"Am I on my way back to shore?"

Whether you've arrived here directly from Point 5: Test the Water, after dipping your oar and found that to be sufficient, or from Point 6: Ride the Wave, after holding a bigger boundary, *you're done for now*. The head-rush is dissipating. It's time to row into the sunset.

Point 7: Head for Shore is about disengaging from the scene to get a sense of closure. The obvious way to head for shore is to extract yourself from the location of your educational boundary experience and physically leave. You can excuse yourself, shake hands, hug, gather your things, wave good-bye—whatever is appropriate for the situation—and exit. Separate yourself from the scene, even if only for a while.

This Point acknowledges a clear ending of the journey of Points 1 through 6. Leaving the scene after the situation has played out invites calmness to make an appearance, gives the overwhelm a chance to fade, and allows your boundary lesson to enter the past tense. *It happened.* Which means *it's over.* Doing this Point is of particular importance if the previous Points took place with high emotion. We can't sustain high emotion healthily for long periods. Get some distance.

If you're done but the person you're interacting with isn't, you likely still have options. Depending on the situation, you might reschedule the conversation to continue later, announce you need a break, or simply say you need to go but will be in touch.

If you decide you need to remain in the situation physically after you rode the wave (or waves) of holding your personal boundaries, you can explore ways to gain the benefits of closure by retreating in other ways—for instance, by withdrawing emotionally, being quiet, or taking a backseat to the continued proceedings going on around you. At some point, you'll be done physically in that situation. Then it's time to head on out.

As you practice Point 7: Head for Shore, swagger like an old sea dog. You've earned it.

Chapter 8
Point 8: Dock Party

"Where's the cooler?"

Congratulations! No matter what happened as you went through the first seven Points, if you approached the process with the honest willingness to learn, *you succeeded*. Even if your accomplishment feels small. Even if your progress consisted only of being aware, for the first time ever, that you were actually in the midst of a boundary-challenging situation. *That's fabulous!* We'll celebrate that.

Celebration begins with acknowledgment. As you reach

the dock and climb out of your boat, while you're still fresh from the experience, take a moment to see if you can clarify what you learned. Tune in. What, exactly, are you celebrating here? Speak your accomplishment out loud, if you're so inclined. Tell someone else as well, if you know someone who will see the accomplishment as the progress it certainly is.

Point 8: Dock Party is about the practice of positive reinforcement. Acknowledgments that include rewards motivate progress. Please don't skip this Point. Devise a way to reward yourself that feels appropriate. Experiment to find celebratory elements that mean something positive to *you*. Your celebrations don't need to be large or cost money, although they can. They don't need to take any more time than you want them to. The goal here is to promote a *feeling* of being rewarded for your honest efforts. This encourages you to make more honest efforts.

Here are some celebration ideas: Go somewhere purely for fun (favorite cafe, walk in the woods, bookstore, best friend's house). Treat yourself to something you love (bubble bath, ebook, comic book, tattoo, office supplies, favorite album, curling up with a new novel). Celebrate with others who support your progress (call a friend, invite someone over for lunch, email your pals, dance with your neighbor, host a game night). Do something both fun and unusual (art night with creative friends, adventure to secondhand stores on the other side of town, order something new at the coffee shop or the office supply store). You know best what feels like a healthy reward to you. Curate a list somewhere so it's handy.

In Point 7: Dock Party, you demonstrate your love and appreciation for yourself by giving your accomplishment space to rumba.

Chapter 9
Point 9: Boat Maintenance

"How can I make my boat more seaworthy?"

Whew! You made it through. The reward was sweet and the next boundary alarm is still on the horizon.

But there's more to do? Yup.

Here's the thing: Holding your personal boundaries is never going to be finished. Knowing how to create and maintain healthy boundaries is a skill set to be used for a lifetime. So the better shape these tools are in, the easier they are to use. *Easy to use,* in this context, means the Steadying Points feel *natural* and *automatic*. This happens by repeatedly practicing the Points to hard-wire the experience, including doing this last Point of maintenance to gain the advantages of building mastery and keeping your boat shipshape.

Point 9: Boat Maintenance is all about evaluation, review, and preparation for the next time you'll venture into territory requiring a boundary to be held. For example, if you notice that one Point in particular tends to be problematic for you, what's the repair? What if you do great with Points 1 to 5, but consistently get hung up on Point 6 when it's time to speak out and ride a bigger wave?

If your boundaries are unhealthy in a bunch of different situations, practice of any kind will move you forward and start making things easier. If your boundaries are fine in most areas, but iffy when it comes to certain situations or certain people, you can focus on conscious practice in those areas.

The experiential learning provided by *conscious* practice trumps everything else. You can't *read* this book enough to achieve healthy boundaries if you're not also *practicing* the Points in real life in real time. Without the *doing,* and the learning that comes from feeling the signals in the moment, your default settings around boundaries are less likely to shift.

Below is a list of automation and mastery tools. Start with the ones that most appeal to you. As you master a tool, move on to another one. You may find that different methods work better for you in different situations. You can zero in on a particular issue, or proactively up your game across the board by trying them all.

Grab your comfy overalls and a sandpaper block. Now's your chance to level up.

Memorize the 9 Steadying Points

Although reading and memorizing alone won't make the ultimate difference, memorizing the 9 Steadying Points, including their order and the question associated with each Point, makes them more likely to be accessible when needed. Memorization of the Points can create a positive cascade effect such that as soon as you become aware you're in Point 1: Check the Weather ("What's rocking my boat?"), you remember how to move through the remaining Points, like tapping the first domino to topple the entire row.

Use the Handy Boundaries Reminder Tool

In the next chapter of this guide there's a link to the book bonuses page online, where you can access a handy reminder tool in different formats, including a PDF to print for hard-copy reminders. Stash reminders in your wallet, purse, desk drawer, back pocket—wherever makes sense for you to have the info when you need it most. Stick a copy on the fridge for the family to use. Tack the handy reminder to your bulletin board at work.

You can also bookmark the online bonuses page to access it quickly from your phone or other device, making the 9 Steadying Points immediately available at a glance in situations where boundary encouragement is needed and you have internet access, like during phone calls, in meetings, at a party, or while home for the holidays. A glance at the reminder tool on your phone beneath the edge of a conference table or dining table, or in a locked bathroom stall, may be all you need as a prompt to take a deep breath and shift your view of the situation to little boats, whose feet are where, and your options for self-care.

The handy reminder's visual associations of graphic images for the 9 Steadying Points and their questions can help the concepts stick so you'll gradually remember them on your own more easily when needed.

Know Yourself

Self-knowledge is power. As you practice holding your boundaries, try to notice patterns around what sets off your alarms. You may already be aware of particular situations or people that tend to rock your boat. When you know an upcoming situation will likely be a boundary challenge for you, you can prepare in order to better support yourself. Review your healthy boundary tools, get a good night's sleep, wear clothes that help you feel good about yourself—do whatever works for you to be ready and steady in your little boat. Personalized advance planning can diminish the negative effects of known or potential boundary threats.

You can also plan in advance what you'll do at your dock party at Point 8 to make the celebration meaningful for you. Every amount of practice, no matter what the outcome, warrants your acknowledgment and applause.

Close the Gaps

Sometimes just being aware of which Points tend to cause you to ditch the process, or to forget you even *have* a process, can make a difference.

One way to gauge your progress with the 9 Steadying Points is to become aware of the time it takes you to move through the earliest Points. Do you get through the first three Points automatically, but then Point 4: Get Your Bearings takes forever, even when you manage to remember in the moment what that Point is?

You can set small goals for yourself to gradually increase your in-the-moment awareness. For example, you might aim to decrease the time it takes you to move through the first four Points.

But be reasonable and patient with yourself. If you consistently test the waters with ease in Point 5 by doing tiny, toe-dipping experiments, but shy away from riding Point 6's waves, even when you know it would benefit you, that's okay. Keep practicing the Points you *can* do. Over time, as your tiny experiments add up, what once seemed like an enormous wave will start to seem approachable, and suddenly there you are, standing up for yourself with the courage of a wave-rider.

Arrange for Back-Up

When faced with a major wave situation guaranteed to challenge your ability to remain true to yourself, but you still want to go there, consider asking for help rather than rowing in the opposite direction. If the benefits on the other side of the wave are substantial and motivating enough to make the risk worthwhile, what type of support would make it safe enough for you? How much can you tailor support to your specific needs? Who can you enlist to help?

A friend of mine planned a trip back home to visit his family—a visit he knew would be emotionally difficult for him. He asked his best friend to go along (and even paid for her plane ticket). She had one job for the duration of the trip: to remind him to breathe. That simple support went a long way toward helping him remain in his own boat during the visit.

Consider buddying up with someone you trust and

supporting each other in the practice of building healthy boundaries. Or ally with a guide or advisor with professional experience. Come up with creative ways to manage boundary support in challenging situations. For example, you and a friend who also knows about the 9 Steadying Steps can use prearranged hand signals—a display of fingers to indicate the Point number to focus on in the moment. Or a touch to the chest could be a reminder to each other to take a deep breath.

Role-Play Practice Together

Role-playing potential boundary-challenge situations can be a powerful way to embody habits of awareness around self-care and authentic expression. With a friend (or friends), set up scenes that approximate circumstances where you want to have more confidence with your boundaries, and act your way through them. Acting out scenarios multiple times helps even more. Depending on the lengths you go to for making the situation feel realistic (dressing the part, simulating the settings, acting with commitment), you can increase mastery in a way that feels safer than the real thing, as a trial run.

Practice with role-play, but don't stop there. Although role-play can ease stage fright and increase your familiarity with the Steadying Points, finding your sea legs in real life is the actual goal.

Consider the Big Bailout

Some situations are unhealthy through and through, and no amount of practicing healthy boundaries with those involved will make them better. This is the time for the personal boundary solution of leaving the situation altogether. If, for example, it's difficult to focus at work because your boss is a bully who shows zero signs of changing, ignores your attempts at self-care, and there's insufficient support in the organization for resolving the issue, consider finding another job. If your partner is emotionally or physically abusive, and attempts on your part to develop healthier boundaries could put you in even more danger, reaching out to people or organizations in positions to help you safely bail out of the relationship could be an effective way to love yourself into better boundaries. Whatever your circumstances, self-loving solutions are possible.

Take the Long View

Be patient. You are a work in progress. Habits can change, but laying in new habits takes attention and willingness over time to make them stick.

If you notice you have a tendency toward unhealthy boundaries (even if only in a limited set of circumstances), it may mean that a particular behavior pattern settled in as a habit in response to something in your environment in the past, maybe during your childhood as part of a survival mechanism. These deeper behavior motivations can be tougher to dismantle. There are plenty of teachers, guides, and counselors with the expertise to help you.

As you become more comfortable with authentic expression and holding boundaries, you'll be confronted with new and different situations requiring you to up your game again and again. Growth shifts the view and brings new factors into play. Maybe you'll go from practicing healthy boundaries in staff meetings at the company where you work in the admin department to figuring out your boundary edges as you lead executives at your own company. Anything is possible. These are habits for a lifetime, and every bit of progress benefits you as it accrues.

What If *You* Are the Boundary Threat?

Yikes! Excuse me? Yes, you read that correctly. What if the boundary that's being threatened belongs to someone you're interacting with and it's *you* who's tromping on *their* truth? Frankly, I don't know anyone who keeps their feet entirely in their own boat 100% of the time. Who's perfect? Not me.

In my experience, boundary issues show up in patterns: *this* type of situation tends to trip me up around maintaining my own boundaries, and *that* type of situation typically plonks my feet into other people's boats, unsettling the boundaries they're trying to maintain. For example, I used to have a pattern where if I felt ignored—*even when I wasn't*—I would jump in with both feet and assume things that weren't true. Not good. What *is* good is that after I identified *feeling ignored* as a trigger, I committed to repairing that habit and learned over time how to de-trigger it.

How does one go about de-triggering an unwanted response? There are lots of ways, including working with a good counselor. De-triggering might involve excavating the underlying reason to understand how and why the trigger was initially established. Many of my triggers were set up during childhood, back when I was (as all children are) unconsciously just trying to survive in relationship with the adults who controlled pretty much everything.

Many of my initial triggers were around being a highly sensitive person, an introvert, and empathic—ways of being that society considered not-normal or less-than. Associating with other people who shared my traits, and learning more about the positives of who I am naturally, helped to flip the scripts in my subconscious and reduce related triggers.

Other options for reducing unhealthy knee-jerk reactions around boundaries include support groups, self-esteem and self-empowerment books (see the Further Resources section), workshops and courses, coaching, and body-centered therapies. How could you learn more about managing *both* sides of the healthy boundary equation—keeping other people's feet out of your boat, and keeping your own feet out of other people's boats? What type of support attracts you?

A hugely beneficial practice to develop if you realize you tend to put your feet in other people's boats is to see how much time you can insert between a trigger and your response. I've had great success with this method, as have other people I've talked with about trigger responses. Many years ago, when I first started trying to work with triggers, the time span between a trigger and my unhealthy reaction was instantaneous. So I made it a game to see how much time I could allow after the trigger before I reacted. At first, for a long time, it was still *no time*, and the best I could do was notice I'd tripped a trigger and notice my immediate unhealthy reaction. Gradually, as I kept practicing awareness around the issue, I moved from reacting immediately to responding thoughtfully. Eventually, I could pause and reflect when triggered. I could *decide* how to respond, either while still in the moment or after taking the time I needed to process things. Triggers happened less and less frequently, and became more of a source of information about my own self-growth needs—signals alerting me to opportunities for healing and personal growth.

The 9 Steadying Points also work as a practice if you're the one making waves. Start as usual at Point 1 and Check the Weather ("What's rocking my boat?"). Does something feel not-right about the moment? *I don't feel so good now. What's going on?* Proceed to Point 2 and Stay in Your Own Boat ("Am I sitting by myself in my own boat?"). *Oh, crap. I'm the one who's shouting.* Do Point 3 and Stop Rowing ("Have I gathered my oars?"). *I'll close my mouth now and sit down. Sheesh. This again.* And so on through the next Points. Please don't forget the acknowledgment and celebration of Point 8: Dock Party. Even if you were the perpetrator, practicing in earnest how to be less of one is definitely cause for celebration.

Boat Maintenance is the last of the 9 Steadying Points. Now that you've been introduced to the entire process, you can adopt it as your own. With a willing heart, make a decision to honor your own boat and the boats of those around you. The rewards are safe passage, clearer communication, deeper connections, authentic expression, and the power to create the life you want.

Handy Boundaries Reminder Tool

When you're in the midst of a tense interaction and your mind blanks, how do you remember your options for self-care? Grab the handy boundaries reminder tool!

Visit the book bonuses page at gracekerina.com/books/personal-boundaries-for-hsps-bonuses to access the reminders tool (shown below) as a PDF to print and stash in pockets, wallets, purses, desk drawers, or on the fridge. You can also bookmark the bonuses page as a digital reference of the 9 Steadying Points.

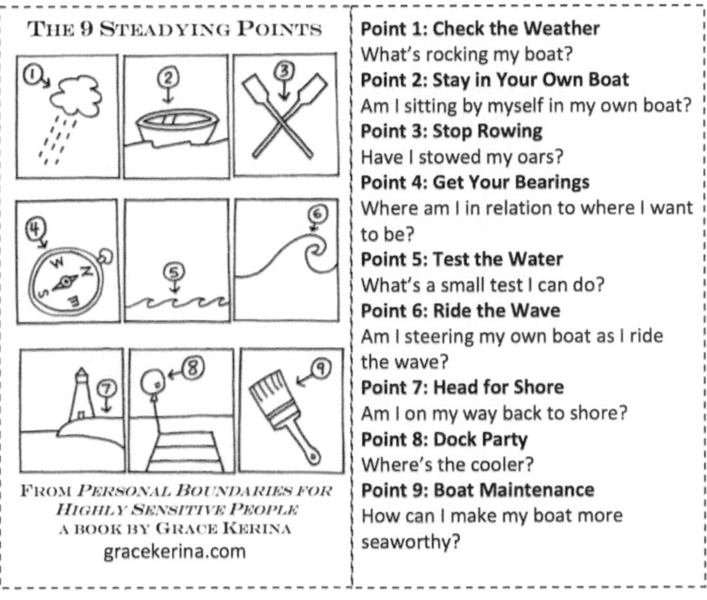

Further Reading

If you want to dive deeper into the world of boundaries, you can pick from many wonderful books currently available. Back at the beginning of my quest to learn how to hold true to myself in relationships, the books listed below helped me immensely.

- *Boundaries: Where You End and I Begin*, by Anne Katherine
- *How to Live with an Idiot: Clueless Creatures and the People Who Love Them*, by John Hoover
- *How to Work for an Idiot: Survive and Thrive Without Killing Your Boss*, by John Hoover
- *Passionate Marriage: Keeping Love and Intimacy Alive in Committed Relationships*, by David Schnarch (Chapter 2 and Chapter 12 provide key concepts about boundaries)
- *Where to Draw the Line: How to Set Healthy Boundaries Every Day*, by Anne Katherine
- *Why Talking Is Not Enough: 8 Loving Actions That Will Transform Your Marriage*, Susan Page (Great tools for any relationship, not only romantic relationships)

Thank You and Bon Voyage

Thank you for being here and for reading this book. Feedback is so helpful for me and for other potential readers. If you have a moment, would you be willing to leave an honest review on Amazon or Goodreads, or mention the book wherever you like to share things with your people? Your support is much appreciated!

As I wrote this book, I pictured you. Our conversations in my head lasted much longer than the size of this book implies. In my mind's eye, I waved my hands and paced as I told you about times I failed *yet again* to protect my boundaries or to respect someone else's boundaries—like when I boarded the boat of the person I loved most and ended up sopping wet when they made me walk the plank. I really enjoyed those conversations with you. They clarified my journey. They helped me make peace with my own past and realize how far I've come in my ability to stand up for myself. Thank you for listening.

I believe you are up to the task of championing your true self. Voyage safely, but also remember to dream big and have some fun. I love you. I can see you shining from here.

Love, Liberation, and Literature
A Website for Highly Sensing Creators

Will you love yourself, no matter what?

On the Love, Liberation, and Literature website, author Grace Kerina shares inspiration and tools to bring highly sensing explorers and creators home to the safe harbor of the self, where we learn to accept who *we* are and love others as *they* are. Love, Liberation, and Literature offers a resting place that reveals the ways we are not lost.

You'll find resources and stories for creative intuitives, compassionate bookworms, and independent thinkers with strong hearts.

**Visit, explore, subscribe at
gracekerina.substack.com**

Protect Yourself from Negative Reviews

A Mini-Manual for Highly Sensitive Writers

Does the idea of sharing your work in public trigger a panic spiral? Did a negative review crush your spirit and make you feel awful? Has critical feedback made you question your creative vision?

You created from your soul, infused your project with love, and invested your time and energy... then someone trashed your work. *Ouch.* The impacts of negative feedback can be debilitating, triggering feelings of shame, humiliation, and fear, and shutting down creativity.

Protect Yourself from Negative Reviews shows you how to champion your open-hearted creativity *and* participate in a marketplace that invites criticism.

Learn transformative mindset shifts and practical steps to gain control of your experience around reviews and resolve the conflict between the drive to share and the need to self-protect.

Available in ebook and paperback

About the Author

Grace Kerina has actively championed highly sensitive people since 2008, through her articles and books, her work as an editor and writing coach, and as the author of literary fiction featuring highly sensitive, creative main characters. She writes novels as Alice Archer. To find out more, visit her website:

Love, Liberation, and Literature
gracekerina.substack.com

9 781734 249378